# Life In The Sandbox

Vol. 1

# 7 Ways to Move Forward

By Noelle Federico

FIRST EDITION

© 2025 by Noelle Federico

All rights reserved. No part of this book may be reproduced without the permission in writing from the author, except by a reviewer who may quote brief passages in a review with appropriate credit; nor may any part of this book be reproduced, stored in a retrieval system, or transmitted in any form or by any means-electronic, photocopying, recording or other-without permission in writing from the publisher.

For information or permissions write:

Wonder Works Studio (a div of Fortunato Partners Inc)
Publishing Division
P.O. Box 342
Fairfax, VT 05454


Cover Design by Pam Smith | Creative Pear Marketing
Formatting by Newbern Consulting, LLC
Back Cover photo by Andrew Cate Photography, VT

ISBN# 978-1-7359355-2-2

# Dedication

- For GOD who makes WAYS where there are no ways…always.

- For my husband, John and my son, Antonio for loving me through all the seasons and for making sure that I never, ever give up—so much still to be done and no better people to do it with – I love you more.

- For Kalli—love you honey.

- For Sedrik, Pam and Kim H.—thank you for always helping me bring my ideas to life—XOXO.

- To Mark for ALL the things--I am eternally grateful for you. XOXO

- For Bryan and all the people in his world…SPJ, Taylor et al. Thank you for making the last 8 years of my life such a magical and blessed time. You all have my love and gratitude…always.

- For Tracy, Rodney, Miranda, Debi, Keely, Selena, Jean, Paula, Marie, Cassandra, Kim, Karen, Kirsten, Stacey and Pam…thank you for being my lifetime friends. I love you all so much.

- For Kyley, Anastasia and Andi thank you for sharing your magic with me. XOXO

- For my friend Kristina and all of the women in my life now because of her…thank you for reminding me of who I am and what I came here to do…cheers to us and all the good that we will bring into the world. Love you. XOXO

**And to the WARRIOR in all of us, who keeps GOING even when we'd rather not. Keep going!**

# Table of Contents

| | |
|---|---|
| Introduction | 5 |
| Building Your Sandcastle: take responsibility for your life | 8 |
| Don't Cry Over Spilled Sand... get over things and move on | 15 |
| Stop Fighting Over the Sand Toys... conserve your energy, pick your battles. | 24 |
| Build On Solid Ground—establish a solid foundation & get priority in order | 36 |
| Don't Be Afraid to Make a Mess— life is a flow not a balancing act. | 47 |
| When Needed Level the Sand and Start Over—get rid of what isn't working | 58 |
| Remember to Have Fun & Start Digging!! --lighten up, include others and get in action | 69 |

# Introduction

Well, here we are together again for my 6th book, imagine that?

After 56 years on the planet, I have determined that what most people and a lot of business people are lacking is a strategy and an action plan. I have met so many incredible people that are stuck in the middle of their own bullshit, unable to free themselves from the attitudes, habits and behaviors that are holding them back. It is truly heartbreaking to watch folks drowning in their own ineffectiveness and excuses. So, heartbreaking in fact, that after 30 years of coaching people I have stopped being willing to do that work as "coaching".

I have determined that in fact, I am not a 'coach'—I am more like a stick of dynamite that will drop underneath you and quite literally BLOW you up out of your apathy and complacency.

A kinder name for me, I decided, is a Strategist.

This month I made the decision to 'retire' from my larger corporate consulting clients in April and pivot into helping solopreneurs, entrepreneurs and small businesses create strategies and action plans that will ACTUALLY move the needle.

I will be 57 this August and plan to live over 100 years—so we'll estimate that I have about

50 plus years left here on this earthly plane and in that time, I want to help as many women and small business people as I can to MOVE FORWARD from where they are to where they want to be.

This book is meant to be a quick, simple and impactful read to get you thinking about where you are now and what you have to do to MOVE forward.  As all my books, it is designed so that you can read it quickly if you wish.  You can also open it to any of the 'ways' and be impacted.

Additionally, it has pages for you to write your own notes.  I believe that my books ought to be 'working' books and to that end there is an 'action' item at the end of each section should you choose to make use of the material herein.

On social media you can find us as 'The Strategy Playground"—hence this Vol. 1 of what will be the "Life in the Sandbox" series—designed to be impactful with a fun twist—Life is what you make it.

What you do next is up to you.

Cheers to you,

Noelle
March 15, 2025

"We keep moving forward, opening new doors, and doing new things, because we're curious and curiosity keeps leading us down new paths."

- Walt Disney

## Building Your Sandcastle: take responsibility for your life

You are the one responsible for your life. The sooner you accept that and operate from it, the better your quality of life will be.

The blame game? Useless. It keeps you stuck, drains your energy, and changes nothing. Newsflash: The only thing you can control is yourself. That's it.

If you want to move forward, you must manage the narrative—and that means **zero room for blame.** Your life, your business, your relationships, your bank account, your success (or lack of it)—all of it is on you. **Period.**

If you want **something NEW and DIFFERENT**, then own where you are right now. No blaming. No excuses. No waiting for the perfect moment.

Life is messy. I get it. **Been there. Done that.** I've been broke, bankrupt, abused, betrayed. I raised a child on my own without a dime of child support. I survived three car accidents that should have ended me. All the things. **So what?** I'm still here. I found a way to **thrive** through all of it. I forgave, I released, and I moved the hell on.

People betray you. Opportunities get missed. Chaos shows up uninvited. **So what?** What matters is **how YOU respond.**

No one is coming to save you. No magical shortcut will suddenly appear. **The Easy Button only exists at Staples.** In the real world, you have to make changes and **do the work** on yourself. You want different results? **Then create a strategy, take action, and move.**

**Build Your Own Sandcastle**

If your life is a mess, it's because:
- ☑ You built it without a plan.
- ☑ You ignored the cracks.
- ☑ You let someone else kick it over.

Whatever happened, **it's still yours to fix.**

Sitting around whining about how awful it looks won't rebuild it. **Roll up your sleeves, get strategic, and start constructing something better.**

## Taking Responsibility looks like:

- **No more excuses.** The moment you stop babbling on about why things didn't work and start figuring out how to make them work is the moment everything changes.
- **Stop waiting for permission.** Too many people sit around waiting for the right moment, the right sign, the right partner, the right idea. Stop that. Decide and move.
- **Drop the victim mindset.** Life and Business are what you make them. Successful people don't waste time crying over things—they re-evaluate, adapt, adjust, and keep going.
- **Own your decisions.** Every choice you've made has led you to this moment. That's not good or bad—it just is. If you want things to be better, make better choices.

# Action Item:

Write down the five biggest complaints you have about your life or business right now. Next to each one, write down what YOU will do to change it.

# Notes:

# Notes:

"You never know how strong you are until being strong is the only choice you have."

—Bob Marley

## Don't Cry Over Spilled Sand: Get Over Things and Move On

Life is going to knock over your sandcastle at least a few dozen times or more. This is a fact. Your future will be determined by your ability to move on.

Where people get stuck is when they continue to dwell on aspects of the past and when they continue to live in old narratives that no longer serve them. We are often trapped in our own minds by stories from the past that we continue to tell ourselves as if they were the truth about us in the present day.

*An example of this would be if you suffered a relationship heartbreak when you were a child and you told yourself that you would never give your whole heart again because it would lead to the same heartbreak --then you vowed never to suffer like that in the future. Fast forward to a 35-year-old commitment-phobe who can't make a relationship work.*

*WHY? The old 'story' is still in there running under everything like a worn out 45 record—*

***old, scratched and useless yet still playing and influencing the current situation.***

Things will happen. Your feelings will get hurt. People will disappoint you. Deals will fall through. Clients will ghost you. Someone might take credit for your idea. Someone else may talk behind your back. You'll make a rash decision, and it won't work the way you want. It's OK. I am of the mind that everything happens for a reason and that everything is designed to teach us something and elevate us.

I am also of the mind that everything is always working for the GOOD even when we cannot see it. That is my personal belief, and it serves me well and has enabled me to transmute the most hellish experiences into the biggest blessings.

What you focus your energy on you will get more of. When life is disappointing it is OK to feel the feelings of the moment, simply don't get lost in them. Don't invite them in for espresso and a scone—don't dwell—keep it moving—keep doing the next thing.

When my mother died rather unexpectedly during the pandemic I could have allowed that to stop me and stop my work of helping people—I could have allowed my sadness to kill my generous spirit—I could have rallied against God and acted as if I were a victim of circumstance. I did not choose that.

I understood that my mother had her own journey and that she was responsible for the choices in her life. We can't fix or save other people. Truly we cannot-- and believe me in the last 56 years I have tried!!!

Sadness came and I moved with it and through it—I didn't sit in it like a pool and let it drown me. I cried and I worked. I cried and I vacationed. I cried and I wrote and did my live show. I kept moving. I did not let my feelings stop me—nor did I try to suppress them.

**This is KEY**—HAVE your feelings and keep moving—the spilled sand doesn't have to stop you—pick up your shovel and keep playing, keep building, keep going.

**Also KEY**—you must forgive yourself and others for all the 'things'—the act of forgiveness is FOR YOU, not for 'them'.

Carrying resentment is like dragging a suitcase through quicksand—it just keeps pulling you down. Drop it. All of it. Not for them. For you.

Just let it go. If we have learned anything in these last years it is that life is shorter than we might imagine, and we must not waste one second of it living lives that we don't love.

Some people will spend years—or their entire lives—fixated on what went wrong, rehashing it, reliving it, letting it define them. That's a choice, and it's not a great one. Wasting time weeping over spilled sand does nothing except keep you stuck in the mess.

Here's a truth: things will go sideways at times. Circumstances will occur that you did not plan for.

What separates the people who move forward from the ones who stay stuck is their ability to let things go, adapt, keep moving and creating.

## Moving On Looks Like:

- **Acceptance is power.** You can't change the past. You can, however, decide what you do next.
- **Let go or be dragged down.** Clinging to the injustice of a situation won't make it right. It will only steal your energy and focus.
- **Separate facts from feelings.** You *feel* betrayed. You *feel* like it's unfair. That may all be true, but none of it changes what is. See things as they are, not worse than they are.
- **Stop telling the story.** Every time you repeat what happened to you, you anchor yourself deeper in it. Drop the old story, create and insert a NEW story and watch how quickly things shift.
- **Redirect your energy.** Instead of being mad about what happened, get obsessed with your next move. Forward momentum is the fastest way to take your power back.

# Action Item:

Write down something that's been holding you back because you haven't let it go.

1. **What happened?** (Stick to the facts.)
2. **How much energy have you wasted on this?**
3. **What would be possible if you stopped focusing on it?**
4. **What's one action you can take *today* to move forward instead?**

At the end of the day, you either have RESULTS or NO RESULTS.
Move on.

# Notes:

# Notes:

"Pick your battles. You don't have to show up to every argument you are invited to."

-Mandy Hale

## Stop Fighting Over the Sand Toys: Conserve Your Energy, Pick Your Battles

One of the fastest ways to drain yourself is to get caught up in every little skirmish, argument, or situation that truly doesn't matter. A lot of us waste an insane amount of time and energy worrying about and fighting over things that, in the grand scheme, won't create forward movement.

Whether in business or life, too many people are spending their days trying to control outcomes, correct others, or make sure everyone plays by their version of the rules. Here's a truth: you don't have that kind of power, and trying to force things to go your way will only exhaust you.

Your energy, words and thoughts are your most valuable resources. Every single day you get to choose what you focus on, what you think about and what you give a voice to.

It's like karmic currency, and how you spend it determines what you end up with as a result. If you spend it in pointless conversations or arguments, chasing after people, or trying to force something to happen, you're essentially throwing your "currency" away. Think about that for a moment—how are you spending your days and nights right now? What are you focusing on and how is that working for you?

**Leave Crazy to the Crazies**

I've said it before, and I'll say it again—leave crazy to the crazies. Some people thrive on drama, and they love nothing more than pulling you into their chaos. They create problems where there are none. They instigate, manipulate, and act out, just to get a reaction.

Guess what? They don't deserve your energy.

As Mel Robbins says, "LET THEM."

It's easy to fall into the trap of engaging and reacting—especially if you're a fixer or a problem solver. You think if you just explain one more time, or prove your point, or defend yourself, you'll finally get through to them. Spoiler alert: you won't. People like this don't want a resolution. They want attention. They want to keep the cycle going because that's what fuels them.

So, the best thing you can do? **Exit the game.**

Refuse to react. Let them throw their tantrums. Let them act like children fighting over sand toys. You? You have no time to waste because you are busy creating a life that works.

**Detach from Outcomes & Protect Your Peace (at all costs!!!)**

Many, many battles are fought internally. People get so emotionally attached to how they *think* things should go that they exhaust themselves fighting against reality.

Business owners do it all the time—they cling to an idea that isn't working, keep offering a product no one wants, or try to make a bad partnership succeed. They force things instead of recognizing when to pivot.

The same thing happens in personal relationships. Someone disappoints you, and instead of accepting that they are who they are, you fight to change them. You battle against what is, trying to get a different result.

You have to learn to **detach from the outcome**. This doesn't mean you don't care about what happens—it means you don't waste your energy trying to control things beyond your reach.

The moment you stop fighting what is and start focusing on what's *next*, you'll experience a level of peace you never imagined. In the Bible it is called, "a peace that passes understanding"—it means that nothing can shake you.

**Respond, Don't React**

Not every comment, email or text deserves a response. Not every challenge requires engagement. Nobody ever 'wins' in an argument because when people are in that reactive state no real harmony can happen, no real solutions can be found in that high emotional state—nothing good happens there. Nothing.

People who are always in fight mode—who have to prove they are right, who can't stand to let something go—are the ones who burn out quickest. The need to constantly battle eats away at their energy, their peace, and ultimately, their results.

I have learned that **one of the best ways to diffuse an attack is to refuse to engage**. When someone tries to provoke you, don't react—respond strategically or, even better, don't respond at all.

Silence is powerful. So is walking away. So is deciding that your energy is too valuable to waste.

One of my favorite things to say when someone is pushing for a fight is, *"Perhaps you are right."* And then I move on.

Letting people *think* they've won doesn't cost you a damn thing. But engaging in their battle? That will cost you your peace, your productivity, and your time.

## Stop Trying to Fix & Save Everyone

If you're a natural fixer, I get it. For years, I took on everyone's problems like they were my personal responsibility. My son, my family, my clients—I felt like I had to make everything right for them.

The problem? **It's exhausting.**

People have to learn their own lessons. You cannot carry them. You cannot force them to see what they are not ready to see. You cannot save people from themselves.

If someone wants your help, they will ask. If they don't? Leave it alone.

This one shift—**only offering help when it is asked for**—will give you so much of your energy back.

**Stand Down When Necessary**

Sometimes, the strongest move you can make is to step back. The military uses the term "stand down" to mean withdrawing from combat, giving soldiers time to rest and recover. The same principle applies to your life and business.

There are times when **pushing harder won't fix the situation**. You've done all you can. You've given it your best effort. Now, it's time to back off and let things unfold as they will.

Standing down doesn't mean you've lost. It means you're smart enough to know when to conserve your energy.

Remember: **you don't have to fight every battle.**

You don't have to fix every problem.

You don't have to control every outcome.

You don't have to let other people's chaos become your chaos.

## Choosing Your Battles Looks Like:

- **Asking yourself: "Does this actually matter?"** If the answer is no, move on.
- **Knowing that being at peace is more important than being right.**
- **Recognizing when someone is just looking for attention and refusing to engage.**
- **Understanding that your energy is limited**—and using it wisely.
- **Letting people be who they are without wasting time trying to change them.**

# Action Item:

1. Write down three situations that are stealing your energy right now.
2. Ask yourself: Is this worth my time and focus?
3. Decide what battle you are going to drop TODAY.

**Energy spent fighting the wrong things is energy you're not using to build the life and business you want. Stop fighting over the sand toys.**

# Notes:

# Notes:

"True and lasting success is all about taking it to the next level, yet in order to get there we first have to stand on a strong foundation."

-Daymond John

## Build On Solid Ground—establish a solid foundation & get priorities in order

A house built on a shaky foundation will collapse the moment the first real storm comes. The same goes for your life and your business. You can't build anything lasting—whether it's a career, a company, or a relationship—on a weak or unstable base.

People struggle, not because they aren't capable, but because they are stacking their goals on top of chaos, disorganization, and unclear priorities. They try to do *everything* instead of focusing in on a few things, and then they wonder why they're overwhelmed and stuck.

If you start with a shaky foundation, nothing you build will hold up over the long haul.

In life I think a solid foundation is made up of three key things:

1. **Owning your shit**—All of it. Your past, your finances, your habits, your distractions, and your patterns.
2. **Prioritizing what actually matters**—This is not just being busy—it's being strategic.

3. **Doing whatever it takes**—No excuses, no procrastination, no waiting for perfect conditions. Remember you either have a result or you have no result. The story doesn't matter. People start believing their own sad, sorry excuses and that is why they remain STUCK.

Stop running in circles and start putting your focus on what will actually move the needle.

**Step One: Own Your Shit**

There is an incredible amount of power in fully owning everything about your life—the good, the bad, and the ugly. Too many people waste energy trying to cover up their flaws, avoid accountability, or pretend to be something they're not.

Here's the thing: *you cannot rise past what you refuse to own.*

If you want to be successful, you need to start by taking full responsibility for every decision you've made, every distraction you've allowed, and every action you have taken to this point. Time to stop blaming circumstances, other people, or past failures. Accept that wherever you are today is a result of the choices you've made in the past. The good news is that you can start fresh right now.

This isn't about guilt. It's about **power**. When you own it, you can change it.

If you're constantly bouncing from one idea to another, half-assing projects, and never following through, that's on you. If you're overwhelmed because you've let distractions and chaos run your day, that's on you.

When you stop making excuses and fully claim where you are, you gain the power to move forward.

**Step Two: Prioritize What Matters**

People get overwhelmed because they try to focus on everything instead of what is important.

**Not everything deserves your time.**

One of the biggest mistakes I see business owners make is trying to tackle everything at once—launching a new product, overhauling their brand, starting a podcast, growing a social media following, revamping their website—all while trying to maintain what they already have.

Newsflash: *trying to do everything means you do nothing well.*

You need to **get clear on what actually moves the needle** in your life and business and put your energy there. That means:

- **Define your "One Thing."** What's the one goal that, if achieved, will create the biggest impact? Start there.
- **Stop being distracted by shiny objects.** Every new idea, tool, or opportunity isn't worth your time. Focus.
- **Create structure.** Block out time for the priorities that matter. No more "fitting things in."
- **Say no more often.** If it doesn't align with your goals, it's a no.

There's a difference between being **busy** and being **productive**. If you're constantly overwhelmed, it's not because you're doing too much—it's because you're not focusing on the right things.

Get ruthless about what gets your energy.

## Step Three: Do Whatever It Takes

People claim they want success; however they aren't actually willing to do what it takes to get it.

They want the results, but they don't want to:

- Work late nights and early mornings.
- Make the hard decisions.
- Give up things that don't serve them.
- Do the small things consistently –day in and day out.
- Do the tedious, unsexy, uncomfortable work.
- Handle their own past and clear old narratives.
- Push past rejection, self-doubt, and failure.
- Stay committed when it looks like there is no result.

Here's the truth: **you will never achieve extraordinary results by staying in your comfort zone. The only thing happening in the comfort zone is apathy and complacency.**

Success demands sacrifice. It requires you to push beyond your limits, ignore the excuses, and show up for yourself daily—*even when you don't feel like it.*

If things aren't moving the way you want them to, it's because you're not doing enough to create momentum. Momentum is **hard** to create, but once you have it, it becomes unstoppable. And you build it through **consistent**, focused effort—**not when it's convenient, daily no matter what.**

If you're willing to do whatever it takes, you will get what you want. Period.

## Building a Strong Foundation Looks Like:

- **Owning every part of your story**—without shame or excuses.
- Eliminating distractions and getting laser-focused on what actually matters.
- **Creating structure so you stop running in circles.**
- **Getting comfortable being uncomfortable**—because growth is hard.
- **Stopping the endless cycle of starting and quitting**—commit fully.
- **Doing what you said you were going to do**—no matter what.

# Action Item:

1. **Write down the three biggest distractions that pull your focus.**
2. **Make a list of the top five things that actually move your business or life forward.**
3. **Cross-check: How much of your daily energy is spent on distractions vs. priorities?**
4. **Decide on one thing you will remove this week to create more focus.**

# Notes:

# Notes:

Life is a series of natural and spontaneous changes. Don't resist them — that only creates sorrow. Let reality be reality. Let things flow naturally forward in whatever way they like."

- Lao Tzu

## Don't Be Afraid to Make a Mess—life is a flow not a balancing act

Somewhere along the way, someone sold us on the idea that we needed balance—that everything should be orderly with defined edges   That school of thought says we must be in control, portion out activities and glide through life without making a mess. That's complete nonsense.

Real life is messy. Growth is messy. Business is messy. If you're doing anything worth doing, you're going to spill some sand, break some things, and have moments where you feel completely lost in chaos.

You don't have to have it all figured out.

You just **keep moving anyway.**

## Stop Trying to 'Balance' Everything

The idea of "work-life balance" is bullshit in my opinion having been a single mom for 18 years I can promise you that there is no such thing. There is no magical equilibrium where everything gets equal attention, and nothing ever falls through the cracks.

That's not how life works. **Life is a flow.** Some days, work takes the lead. Some days, family takes it. Sometimes, your personal growth requires you to step away from everything else for a while.

Give yourself permission to do what you need to do. It's OK—the balance police are not coming to get you.

Trying to force everything into perfect form will only leave you frustrated, exhausted and feeling bad about yourself. Instead of chasing balance, **start embracing flow.**

There are times when you'll have to go all-in on a big career move. Other times, you'll need to step back and focus on your relationships or your health. When you stop resisting this natural cycle and start working *with* it instead of against it, life gets a hell of a lot easier.

### The Process is Messy—Trust It Anyway

People get stuck when they're afraid to get things wrong. They don't take action because they don't want to make a mess. They hesitate, overthink, and hold themselves back because they believe they need a perfect plan before they can move forward.

That's not how it works.

Everything worth building goes through a messy middle. You don't get to skip that part.

- Businesses don't scale without stumbling through mistakes.
- Relationships don't grow without hard conversations.
- Personal breakthroughs don't happen without discomfort.

I've had plenty of moments where I thought I had failed, only to realize later that I was just in the middle of a process I couldn't fully see yet.

Back in 2016, I had the idea to create a yearly workbook to help people design a better new year. I started working on it, but it never fully materialized. I thought it was a failed idea. Fast forward to 2019, and suddenly, everything clicked. That same workbook—got refined and fully developed—and became something we released every December from 2019 to 2024 for

The Coffee Chat Show** audience.

(**The Coffee Chat Show was my live FB Show that ran from 2014 to 2024 from my page The Working Happy Mom. I retired the show at the beginning of 2025 to fully embrace my pivot into strategy. Old shows can be accessed from my website – www.fortunatopartners.com)

The idea wasn't a failure. It was a process.

At the time, I couldn't see that I wasn't *ready* to create what it would eventually become. There were lessons I needed to learn, experiences I needed to have. It had to take that long.

This is how life works. Sometimes, you're in the middle of something great, and you just don't know it yet.

**Life Will Knock You Around—Keep Going**

In the summer of 2018, I was driving along, minding my own business, when a construction truck and trailer jumped their lane and came at me head-on. I swerved in time to avoid a direct hit, but they still took off the entire driver's side of my brand-new car—including shearing off the wheel. The impact was so forceful that it knocked the three cars behind me off the road as well as left my car hanging over a river with only the front half of the vehicle stabilized. In that moment I had a choice. I chose response vs. reaction and somehow, I got the moonroof open and was able to climb out and down the front of the car. I remain unharmed from that incident because I chose to immediately begin blessing that circumstance and declaring that good would come from it. In my fear and in my weeping and in my shock—I kept declaring the good and good is what came.

That incident could have destroyed me— physically, mentally, emotionally. Yet I refused to allow that. What was meant to harm me ended up blessing me in ways I couldn't have imagined. That moment taught me something I hadn't fully learned before — **I am not in control of everything; HOWEVER, I can <u>always</u> control my responses and how I choose to move forward.**

I don't get to dictate the timeline. I don't get to see the whole plan at once. I don't get to avoid every mess or challenge that comes my way.

Neither do you.

What you *do* get to control is your **response**. Do you freeze? Do you let fear dictate your actions? Or do you keep moving, trusting that—even if it doesn't look like it right now—things are actually working in your favor? Part of that is speaking the good even when things look a mess—you must stand in the face of what it looks like—no matter the shit storm—you must stand in it declaring your intention for the outcome. I have proven this – I have lived through it more than once and I promise you that it works.

This isn't for the faint of heart—there is a level of mastery required to stand in hell and declare that it's paradise—if you are willing to turn your attention consistently to the outcomes that you want to manifest – circumstances will yield. I am living proof of that.

**Stop Multi-Tasking & Start Living**

People love to talk about multi-tasking like it's some kind of superpower. The truth? It's killing your focus and robbing you of being fully present in your own life.

- You half-listen to your kids while scrolling on your phone.
- You check emails while eating dinner.
- You're on a Zoom call while also trying to answer texts.

You think you're being productive, but all you're really doing is giving *everything* half your attention instead of giving *something* your full attention.

If you want to be successful—whether in business, relationships, or personal growth—you have to stop trying to do *everything* at once.

Be where you are.

When you're with your family, be fully there. When you're working, focus on the task in front of you. When you're resting, actually rest—don't half-work while pretending to take time off.

Your life is happening *right now*. Stop missing it.

## Embracing the Flow Looks Like:

- **Letting go of perfection.** Nothing will ever be perfect. Move forward anyway.
- **Trusting the process.** Just because you don't see the whole picture yet doesn't mean it's not coming together.
- **Getting comfortable with making a mess.** Growth is messy. Business is messy. Life is messy. Accept it.
- **Focusing on what matters.** Stop trying to balance everything. Flow with what needs your attention most.
- **Being fully present.** Stop multi-tasking your life away. Pay attention to what's in front of you.

# Action Item:

1. **Write down one area where you're hesitating because you don't want to get it wrong.**
2. **What's one step you can take today to move forward—even if it's messy?**
3. **Identify one place where you can stop multi-tasking and be fully present.**

**Notes:**

**Notes:**

## When Needed Level the Sand and Start Over — get rid of what isn't working

Sometimes you must level the sand and start over and sometimes you need to pour water on the castles that no longer serve you. When something isn't working, and you have done your best to fix it or counsel it or change it – yet it still isn't serving you then **stop trying to force it**. Stop attempting to breathe life into a dead thing. Just as we have to prune trees or pull-out dead bushes, we also have to take these actions in our lives and relationships.

Too many people hold onto things long past their expiration date—jobs that drain them, relationships that deplete them, routines that no longer serve them. They keep showing up, trying to make it work, convincing themselves that if they just push a little harder, stay a little longer, tolerate a little more—it'll get better.

**It won't.**

If something is really broken and no amount of effort is fixing it, **it's time to level the sand and start over.**

## The Courage to Clean House

Starting over doesn't mean you failed. It means you're wise enough to recognize when something is no longer aligned with where you're going.

You can't move into the future you want if you're dragging along the dead weight of the past. That includes:

**\*Relationships that drain you instead of support you**
**\*Business strategies that aren't producing results**
**\*Old habits that keep you stuck in the same patterns**
**\*Thoughts and beliefs that tell you you're not capable of something new**

The hardest part of change isn't the change itself. It's the **decision** to make it.

Once you admit that something isn't working, you have to do something about it. You must face the discomfort of letting go. And that's what keeps most people stuck—**the fear of what happens next.**

They settle for "good enough" because **good enough is comfortable.**

The truth: **Settling is a slow death.** The longer you tolerate things that don't serve you, the more they drain your energy, rob your joy, and prevent you from living the life you desire.

If something isn't right, **fix it or let it go.** Period.

**Your Inventory List—What Stays, What Goes?**

How about doing an inventory of the relationships and alliances in your life? **Who contributes to you, and who takes away from you?**

Everyone you encounter does one or the other.

☑ **Some people add to your life.** They challenge you, support you, push you forward.
✘ **Some people drain you.** They take, they complain, they create chaos.

**The same applies to everything else in your life.**

- Are you keeping a job that makes you miserable because you're afraid of change?
- Are you tolerating a relationship that no longer feels aligned?
- Are you holding onto old behaviors that keep you stuck?
- Are you still clinging to an outdated version of yourself?

If you want a **new** kind of life, it's time to be willing to make **new** decisions. That starts with an honest inventory of **what works** and **what doesn't work**.

It's time to **clean house.**

### Cleaning Out the Fridge—The Hidden Toxicity

Let's talk about toxic thoughts and habits. These are just as damaging as toxic relationships and bad business decisions.

The problem? **They're harder to see.**

- You don't always recognize when your own mindset is holding you back.
- You don't always notice the old stories that keep replaying in your head.

- You don't always see how you're sabotaging your own progress.

Here's how I like to explain it: **Your mind is like a fridge.**

If you leave rotting food in the fridge, it doesn't just sit there harmlessly. **It contaminates everything else.** You can put in fresh, healthy food, but guess what? If the moldy orange is still lurking in the back under the drawer, it's only a matter of time before the new food gets tainted.

Your mind works the same way.

**If you don't clean out the expired, toxic thought patterns, they will contaminate every new thing you try to bring into your life.**

- You'll get a new opportunity and talk yourself out of it.
- You'll start a business and sabotage it with old habits.
- You'll meet someone great and ruin it by repeating past patterns.

If you don't **clear out the old**, the new **won't be able to thrive.**

## Are You Settling for Less Than You Deserve?

Ask yourself: **What are you tolerating that you know deep down isn't okay?**

- Where are you letting things slide that you shouldn't?
- What have you convinced yourself is "fine" when it really isn't?
- What have you accepted because you're afraid to do something different?

Settling feels easier in the moment, but the cost is **huge**.

It drains your energy. It chips away at your self-respect. It keeps you trapped in a life that feels mediocre instead of one that excites you.

There are only two ways out:

**Stop accepting what's unacceptable.** Have the hard conversation. Make the tough decision. Rip the Band-Aid off and move forward.

or

**Change your perspective.** If leaving isn't an option, then shift how you view the situation.

Stop resenting it and start blessing it. Stop seeing it as a burden and start looking for ways to make it work for you.

Either way, **you take back control.**


Everything you want is on the other side of letting go of what's no longer working.

**Have the courage to level the sand and start fresh.**

# Action Item:

**Time to Level the Sand**

1. **Make a list of everything in your life right now that isn't working.** This can be relationships, work situations, habits, thought patterns—anything that feels stagnant or draining.
2. **Decide what needs to go.** Be brutally honest. If something isn't serving you, it's time to release it.
3. **Take one action today to start clearing the sand.** Maybe it's a conversation, maybe it's setting a boundary, maybe it's physically removing something from your space. Do something *now*.

# Notes:

# Notes:

"Happiness is not something ready-made. It comes from your own actions."

- Dalai Lama

**Have Fun and Start Digging!! -- lighten up, include others and get in action**

Life is not meant to be a solitary, exhausting grind. You are not here to suffer, push through, and exist in a constant state of stress.

**You are here to live.** To create. To enjoy. To connect. To build something meaningful.

And yet, so many people are standing on the edge of their own life **waiting.**

- Waiting for the perfect moment.
- Waiting until they feel ready.
- Waiting for things to be easier.

**STOP WAITING. START DIGGING.**

The life you want isn't going to drop out of the sky. It's not going to magically appear when the timing feels right. You plunge your hands in the sand and start creating it.

The time is now.

## Happiness is a Choice—And It's Found in Your Relationships

One of the biggest myths about success is that once you **achieve** something—hit a certain income, get the house, land the deal—you'll suddenly feel **fulfilled**.

That's not how it works.

The **longest-running study on happiness** (Harvard's 85+ year study) has proven one thing over and over again: **our relationships are what make life truly fulfilling.**

Not money.
Not status.
Not achievement.

**People. Connection. Shared experiences.**

Yet, so many people prioritize **everything else** first—only to reach a certain point in life and realize that success without meaningful relationships is **empty**.

The happiest people aren't the ones who "have it all" on paper. They are the ones who:

✓ Have deep, meaningful relationships
✓ Support and uplift others
✓ Give freely without expectation
✓ Laugh often and don't take life so seriously
✓ Focus on what truly matters, not just what society tells them should matter

If you want to build something incredible in your life, **include others in the process**.

Make time for friendships. Prioritize your family. Find people who light you up and **make the effort to keep them close.**

Nothing you build will ever mean as much if you don't have people to share it with.

### The Joy of Kindness—What You Give Comes Back

If you're feeling stuck, frustrated, or uninspired, here's a **simple way to shift everything**:

**Do something for someone else.**

- Buy coffee for the person behind you.
- Send a message to someone letting them know you appreciate them.
- Hold the door.
- Give a genuine compliment.
- Tip a little extra.

You don't need grand, sweeping gestures to make an impact. **Small, consistent acts of kindness change everything.**

They change **your mood**.
They change **your energy**.
They change **how people respond to you**.

**They change YOU.**

When you give freely—without expecting anything in return—you invite **more goodness** into your own life.

It's not magic. It's how energy works.

**What you put out into the world comes back to you.**

If you walk around guarded, cynical, and resentful, life will reflect that right back at you. If you walk around with generosity, openness, and joy, you'll be amazed at how quickly things start to shift.

Want more good things in your life? **Be the person who creates them for others.**


### Stop Overthinking and Start Moving

How many times have you talked yourself out of doing something?

- "What if it doesn't work?"
- "What if I look stupid?"
- "What if I fail?"

What if… you succeed?

What if… you find something amazing?

What if… this is the thing that changes everything?

**You will never know unless you start.**

Don't be one of those people sitting on the sidelines, **paralyzed by fear and overthinking**, instead jump in and figure it out as you go.

You don't need to know **all the steps** right now. You just need to take **the first one.**

**Get in the sandbox. No more excuses! Grab your tools. Start digging.**

# Action Item:

Take one thing you've been overthinking, waiting on, or avoiding—and take **immediate action** on it.

**\*What's something you've wanted to start but haven't?** (A project, a goal, a conversation, a change?)

**\*What's the first, smallest step you can take today?** (Send an email, make a call, write the outline, set the meeting—whatever it is, **do it now**.)

\* **Who can you bring into the process?** (A friend, a mentor, a collaborator, someone who will hold you accountable and make it more fun.)

\* **Do one small act of kindness today**—no matter how simple. Watch how it shifts your energy.

# Notes:

# Notes:

# Life in the Sandbox: Action Plan

*Your Next Steps to Move Forward*

Now that you've made it through *Life in the Sandbox…7 Ways to Move Forward*, it's time to **put everything into action.** Reading is great, but **nothing changes until YOU do something.**

This isn't just another book to sit on your shelf—it's a **blueprint for real movement.** The **smallest step forward beats the best plan that never happens.** Let's get to it.

## Step 1: Take Ownership

◆ Look back at your notes from *Building Your Sandcastle*. What excuses or blame patterns do you need to drop right now? Write down ONE thing you will take full responsibility for today.

◆ Identify ONE action step you can take to reclaim control over your life, business, or mindset. Then—**do it today.**

## **Step 2: Drop the Baggage**

◆ Review *Don't Cry Over Spilled Sand*. What past event, failure, or disappointment is still weighing you down?


◆ Write down what you **choose** to release—and how much energy you'll get back by letting it go.


◆ Burn the paper, rip it up, or throw it in the trash—whatever helps you **symbolically leave it behind.**

## Step 3: Protect Your Energy

♦ *Stop Fighting Over the Sand Toys* reminded you to **choose your battles.** Where are you wasting energy trying to control things that don't really matter?


♦ Write down **one situation** where you will step back and **let people be** instead of engaging in their drama.


♦ Practice **responding instead of reacting** this week and note how it shifts your peace.

## **Step 4: Strengthen Your Foundation**

◆ If you want long-term success, you need solid ground. From *Build on Solid Ground*, list your **top 3 priorities** that deserve your time and attention.


◆ What distractions or unnecessary tasks need to go? **Cross them out.**

## Step 5: Get Comfortable with Messy

◆ Life isn't a perfect balancing act—it's a **flow.** What's one thing you've been **afraid to start because you don't want to "get it wrong"**?

◆ Write it down. Then, take the **first imperfect step forward.**

## **Step 6: Clear the Sand and Start Fresh**

◆ Look at *When Needed, Level the Sand and Start Over*. What in your life or business **isn't working anymore?**

◆ List the things you know you need to **clean out, cut off, or walk away from.**

◆ Pick **one** to take action on this week. No overthinking. Just **do it.**

## **Step 7: Have Fun and Start Digging!**

◆ Happiness isn't about waiting for "one day"—it's about what you **create right now.**

◆ Write down **one small, daily habit** that brings you joy.

◆ Choose **one act of generosity** to do this week for someone else.

## **Final Thought: The Only Way is Through**

Moving forward isn't about perfection—it's about **persistence**. You don't have to get it all right today. You just have to **keep going.**

You are in charge of the life you build.

**Grab your pail and shovel and get to work.**

## About the Author

### Noelle Federico

Noelle Federico is a **business strategist, operations expert, and no-BS problem solver** with over **36 years of experience** helping entrepreneurs, executives, and business owners scale, streamline, and succeed. She **cuts through the noise, eliminates roadblocks, and delivers real-world strategies that create measurable results.**

As the founder of **Fortunato Partners, Inc.,** Noelle has worked across multiple industries—from media and finance to leadership development and corporate consulting. A former **C-suite executive and strategic advisor,** she has helped companies and solopreneurs alike **optimize operations, improve profitability, and build sustainable success.**

Known for her **direct, results-driven approach,** Noelle helps business owners stop spinning their wheels and start executing on what actually moves the needle. She specializes in **clarity, accountability, and action plans that get things done.**

Beyond consulting, Noelle is a **dynamic speaker, writer, and mentor.** She has built a **strong online presence**, reaching over **1.8 million people** through her social media brands. A **certified John Maxwell Team Member** and **licensed Wiley DiSC Partner**, she provides expert-level consulting for individuals and teams.

Her latest book, **Life in the Sandbox… 7 Ways to Move Forward,** is a no-BS guide to getting unstuck, taking action, and making meaningful progress in both business and life.

When she's not **strategizing, advising, or writing,** Noelle enjoys life in Vermont with her family—**always with coffee in hand and a relentless drive to help people unlock their full potential.**

You can visit her at www.fortunatopartners.com

www.ingramcontent.com/pod-product-compliance
Lightning Source LLC
LaVergne TN
LVHW051152080426
835508LV00021B/2592